Crafts for Kids Who Are
LEARNING ABOUT
DINOSAURS

To Evan and Abby

Millbrook Press
A division of Lerner Publishing Group, Inc.
241 First Avenue North
Minneapolis, MN 55401 U.S.A.

Website address: www.lernerbooks.com

Library of Congress Cataloging-in-Publication Data

Ross, Kathy (Katharine Reynolds), 1948–
    Crafts for kids who are learning about dinosaurs / by Kathy Ross ;
  illustrated by Jan Barger.
       p.   cm.
    ISBN: 978–0–8225–6809–4 (lib. bdg. : alk. paper)
    1. Handicraft—Juvenile literature. 2. Dinosaurs—Juvenile literature.
  3. Dinosaurs in art—Juvenile literature. I. Barger, Jan, 1948– ill.
  II. Title.
  TT160.R71223 2008
  745.5083—dc22   2006100645

Manufactured in the United States of America
1 2 3 4 5 6 – JR – 13 12 11 10 09 08

Crafts for Kids Who Are
LEARNING ABOUT
DINOSAURS

KATHY ROSS
Illustrated by Jan Barger

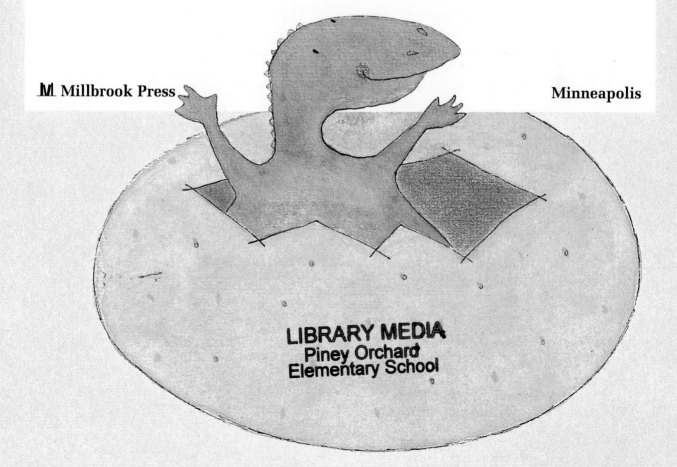

M Millbrook Press

Minneapolis

Table of Contents

Fossil Necklace

No one has ever seen a dinosaur. We learn about them from fossils—bones, tracks, and other traces preserved in rocks.

Here is what you need:

1½-inch (3.8-cm) juice bottle cap

dried coffee grounds

dry rice grains

craft stick for mixing

white craft glue

clear packing tape

colored plastic tape

thin craft ribbon

paper cup

scissors

ruler

Here is what you do:

1. Fill a juice cap with coffee grounds. Pour the grounds into the paper cup.

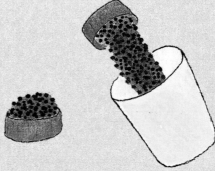

2. Mix in enough glue to hold the grounds together.

3. Press the gluey grounds into the juice cap.

4. Press the rice grains into the grounds to make the dinosaur's bones. Let dry.

5. Wrap the edge of the lid with a strip of colored plastic tape.

6. Cover the fossil with clear packing tape. Wrap the edges around to the back of the lid.

7. Cut a 24-inch (61-cm) length of craft ribbon.

8. Tape the two ribbon ends to the back of the fossil to make a necklace.

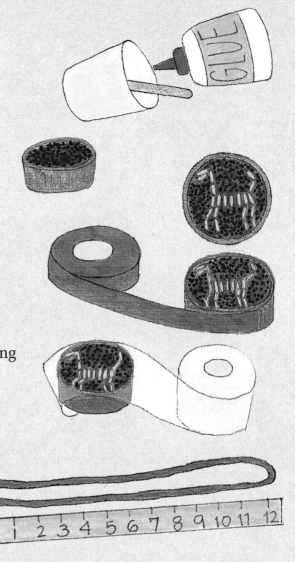

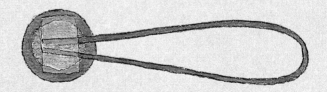

What kind of dinosaur bones are in your fossil?

Leaf-Eating *Seismosaurus*

Some dinosaurs were very large with long necks and tails!

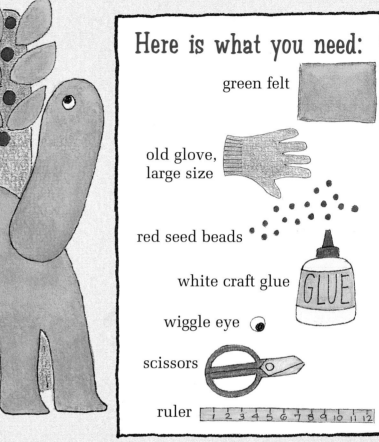

Here is what you need:

green felt

old glove, large size

red seed beads

white craft glue

GLUE

wiggle eye

scissors

ruler

Here is what you do:

1. Cut 30 or more 1-inch (2.5-cm) leaves from the green felt.

2. Glue the leaves to the four fingers of the palm side of the glove to make the tree.

3. Glue red seed beads to the tree for the fruit or flowers.

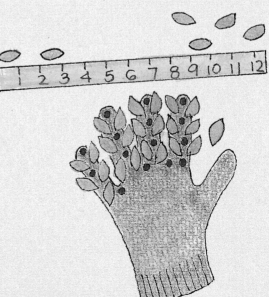

4. Cut a body with a tail and four legs from the felt to fit over the palm of the glove.

5. Glue the body to the hand of the glove below the leaves.

6. Cut a long neck and head from the felt. Glue it to the thumb of the glove so you can move the neck.

7. Glue the wiggle eye to the head of the dinosaur.

To use the puppet, place the glove on your hand. Touch your thumb to your fingers to swing the dinosaur's head back to nibble on the tree branches.

Seismosaurus (SYZ-muh-SAWR-uhs)

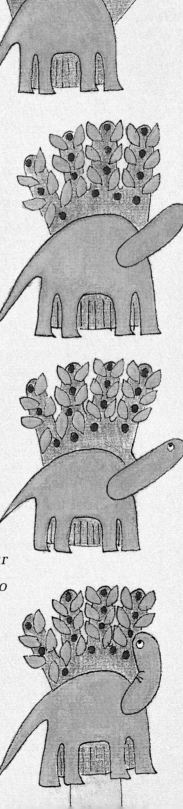

9

Racing *Compsognathus*

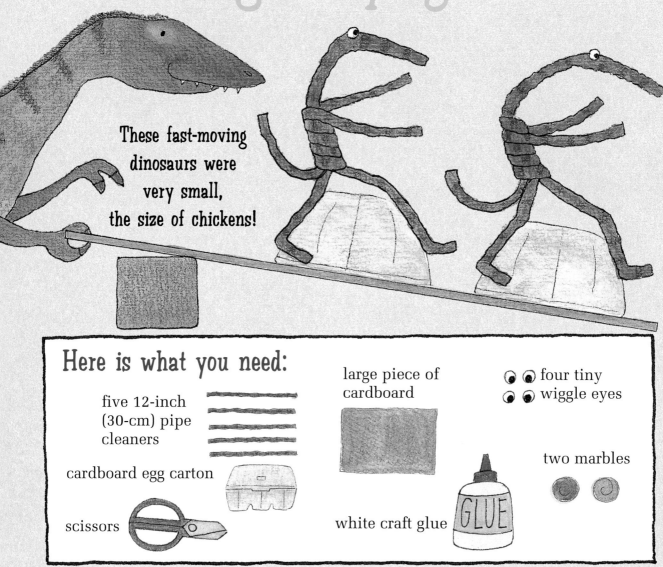

These fast-moving dinosaurs were very small, the size of chickens!

Here is what you need:

five 12-inch (30-cm) pipe cleaners

cardboard egg carton

scissors

large piece of cardboard

white craft glue

four tiny wiggle eyes

two marbles

Here is what you do:

1. Fold a pipe cleaner in half. Curve out the two bottom halves to form running legs.

2. Bend the ends of the legs to shape feet.

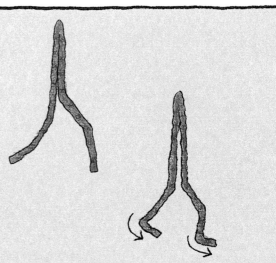

3. Wrap a second pipe cleaner around the middle section. This will thicken the body. Leave the two ends sticking out for the arms.

4. Cut a pipe cleaner in half. Slip one end up through the thick body in back. Let a piece hang down. Curve it out to form a tail.

5. Tip the top of the folded pipe cleaner forward. This is the head.

6. Glue a tiny wiggle eye on each side of the head.

7. Cut a cup from the cardboard egg carton. Glue the *Compsognathus* figure to the top of the cup.

8. Make a second *Compsognathus*.

To race the dinosaurs, place an object such as a block of wood under one end of the cardboard. Place a marble under the egg cup of each dinosaur. At the signal to start, let them go and see which one is the fastest!

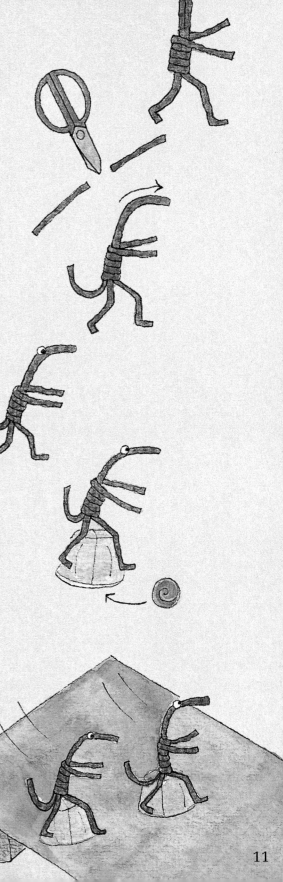

Compsognathus
(KOMP-sohg-NAY-thus)

Hungry *Brachiosaurus*

Brachiosaurus had a long neck. Its neck helped it to reach leaves at the tops of tall trees.

Here is what you need:

two identical 4-inch (10-cm) gift bows

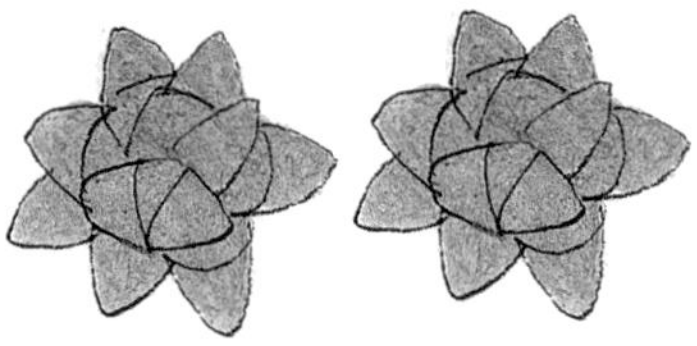

two green four-bump chenille stems

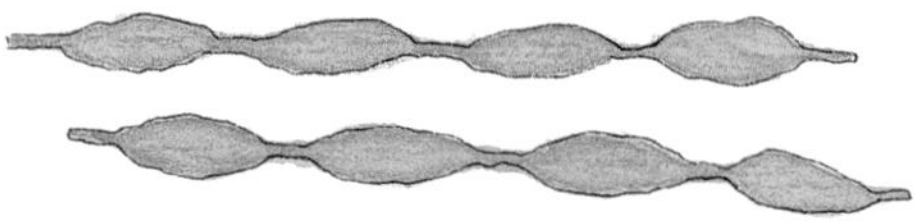

white craft glue

scissors

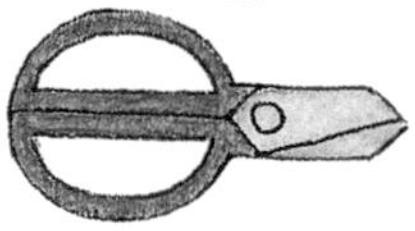

two small wiggle eyes

Here is what you do:

1. Turn one bow so the cardboard square on the bottom is facing up.

2. Glue a four-bump chenille stem onto the cardboard. Two bumps should stick out on one end (this will be the head) and one bump on the other end (this will be the tail).

3. Cut the four bumps from the second chenille stem to make four legs.

4. Bend each bump end to form a foot.

5. Glue the tops of the legs to the cardboard. They should hang down to form legs and feet.

6. Glue the cardboard side of the second bow over the first to form the body. Let dry.

7. Bend the top bump of the neck into a head. Glue on the wiggle eyes.

8. Bend the tail down. (*Brachiosaurus* used its tail for support.)

9. Arrange the legs so that the dinosaur can stand up.

You can make a variety of long-necked dinosaurs using bows of different colors and sizes.

Brachiosaurus
(BRAK-ee-uh-SAWR-uhs)

Bow Tree

Make a tree for your long-necked dinosaurs to nibble on.

Here is what you need:

cardboard paper towel tube

green gift bow

white craft glue

scissors

brown marker or crayon

masking tape

ruler

1 2 3 4 5 6 7 8 9 10 11 12

Here is what you do:

1. Cut a 6-inch (15-cm) piece from the cardboard tube. Cover the outside with 1-inch (2.5-cm) pieces of overlapping masking tape.

2. Color the tape brown. This is the tree trunk.

3. Glue the green gift bow to the top of the tube. It makes the tree's leaves.

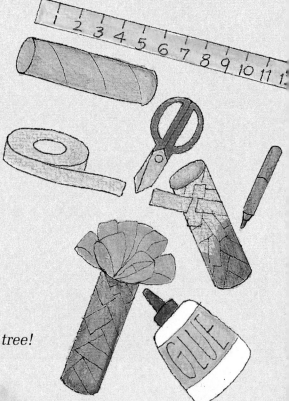

The Brachiosaurus *on page 12 would love this tree!*

Plesiosaurus Bathtub Toy

Here is what you need:

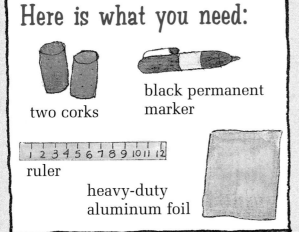

two corks

black permanent marker

ruler

heavy-duty aluminum foil

Reptiles, such as *Plesiosaurus*, swam the oceans during the age of the dinosaurs.

Here is what you do:

1. Tear off a 4-inch (10-cm) strip of aluminum foil.

2. Set the corks on the foil slightly to the right of the center. Wrap the foil around the corks.

3. Squeeze the extra foil together on each end. The longer end will be the neck and head, and the other will be the tail.

4. Draw eyes and flipperlike arms and legs.

This Plesiosaurus *is a great swimmer, so take it in the bathtub with you!*

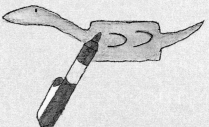

Plesiosaurus (PLEE-see-o-SAWR-uhs)

Grazing Long-Necked Dinosaur Puppet

Here is what you need:

green net
bath scrubby

light-colored,
long-sleeved,
adult T-shirt

scissors

white craft glue

permanent markers

clamp clothespins

rubber band

ruler

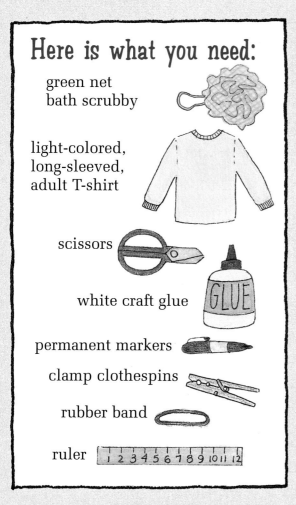

The long-necked dinosaurs needed
a lot of food to survive.

Here is what you do:

1. Cut a back panel, below the arms, out of the shirt.

2. Cut off the bath scrubby rope, leaving a long net tube.

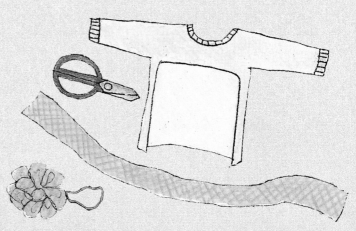

3. Cut five 12-inch-long (30-cm) pieces of net tube to use for the leaves on the tree.

4. Turn the shirt inside out, and glue the neck opening and one sleeve opening shut.

5. Secure the glued edges with clothespins. Let dry.

6. Remove the clothespins, and turn the shirt right side out.

7. Use a brown marker to draw bark on the open sleeve. This will be the tree trunk.

8. Place the five net pieces in the opening at the top of the tree trunk. Secure them loosely with a rubber band around the cuff. Fold the cuff down over the rubber band to cover it.

9. Push the closed end of the opposite sleeve inside itself to form the dinosaur's mouth.

10. Color the mouth with a red marker. Use a marker to draw eyes.

11. Draw the outline of the dinosaur's body and legs on the shirt.

To use the puppet, slide an arm into each sleeve. Hold the tree up. Swing the head of the dinosaur over to the tree to pull a leaf off to munch on. Because the rubber band is loose, the leaves are easy to pull out and replace.

T. rex Collar Clip

Some dinosaurs, such as *Tyrannosaurus rex*, ate other dinosaurs!

Here is what you need:

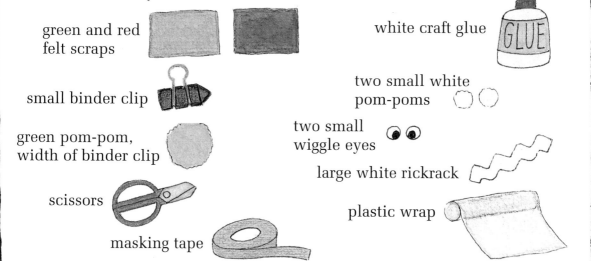

green and red felt scraps

small binder clip

green pom-pom, width of binder clip

scissors

masking tape

white craft glue

two small white pom-poms

two small wiggle eyes

large white rickrack

plastic wrap

Here is what you do:

1. Cover the top and bottom of the clip with a strip of masking tape to create a better gluing surface.

2. Cut two identical rectangles from the green felt large enough to cover the front and back of the clip. Round off the corners.

3. Cut a third rectangle the same size from the red felt.

4. Glue the green rectangles to the top and the bottom of the clip. Make sure the rounded ends are at the opening end of the clip.

5. Fold the red felt in half. Rub glue on the top and bottom of the outside of the felt.

6. Pinch the clip open, and push the folded felt in to form the mouth of the dinosaur.

7. Trim the ends of the felt even with the head.

8. Glue the green pom-pom in between the handles of the clamp at the back of *T. rex*'s head.

9. Cut two strips of the white rickrack. Pinch the clip open. Glue the strips across the top and bottom of the mouth for teeth. Clamp the mouth over a piece of plastic wrap to keep the teeth from sticking together while the glue dries.

10. Glue on the white pom-poms and wiggle eyes.

Be careful not to let T. rex *take a bite out of your collar!*

Tyrannosaurus rex (tih-RAN-uh-SAWR-uhs REKS)

Changing Defenses Dinosaur Puppet

Some plant-eating dinosaurs used shields or spiked tails to protect themselves from meat-eating dinosaurs.

Here is what you need:

adult-size sock

two to four flexible straws

cardboard egg carton

scissors

two large wiggle eyes 👀

white craft glue

four or more clamp clothespins

masking tape

Here is what you do:

1. Glue two wiggle eyes on the toe end of the sock.

2. Cut three attached bumps from the cardboard egg carton.

3. Cut the strip of bumps in half.

4. Glue a strip of bumps to each side of a clothespin. These will be the shields.

5. Use two other clothespins to hold the bumps in place until the glue dries.

6. Attach these shields by clamping the clothespin to the back of the sock puppet.

7. Choose as many straws as you want spikes on a tail.

8. Tape the straws together below the bending tops. Cut each straw top into a point, and spread the spikes out.

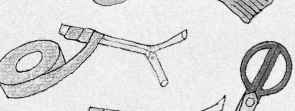

9. Glue the straw tail to one side of a clothespin.

10. Attach the clothespin to the back of your dinosaur to give it a spiked tail.

What other kinds of dinosaur defenses could you make for the dinosaur puppet?

Bone-Headed Dinosaur
Pencil Topper

Pachycephalosaurus had a
thick, bony skull.

Here is what you need:

Styrofoam craft egg

smaller half of plastic
egg that opens

aluminum foil

four straight pins

four large seed beads

pencil

scissors

permanent
markers

Here is what you do:

1. Press the small half of the plastic egg into the Styrofoam egg to create the bony skull.

2. Use the pencil point to poke a hole through the bottom of the foam head.

3. Slip the head over the eraser end of the pencil.

4. Cover the head with aluminum foil. Trim off the excess foil around the pencil.

5. Use the straight pins to attach two seed beads to the head for eyes. Pin two more seed beads for nostrils.

6. You can color the foil with permanent markers.

The bone-headed dinosaurs came with built-in safety helmets!

Pachycephalosaurus (pak-ee-SEF-uh-lo-SAWR-uhs)

Duck-Billed Dinosaur Magnet

The duck-billed dinosaurs had wide, toothless beaks, much like a duck's bill. They used their beaks to scoop up vegetation and grind it with their powerful jaws. *Edmontosaurus* had a plain head. Other duckbills had bony pieces sticking out of their heads.

Here is what you need:

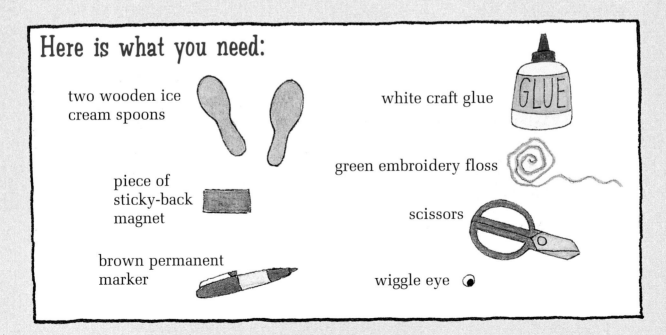

two wooden ice cream spoons

piece of sticky-back magnet

brown permanent marker

white craft glue

green embroidery floss

scissors

wiggle eye

Here is what you do:

1. Glue the eating end of the two spoons together at an angle to form a flat head with the mouth open.

2. Color the head brown.

3. Glue the wiggle eye to the head.

4. Cut several strands of green embroidery floss.

5. Flip the dinosaur over. Glue the floss around the opening so it looks like the dinosaur is eating green vegetation.

6. Press a piece of sticky-back magnet to the back of the head.

Corythosaurus is another duck-billed dinosaur. To make its crest, break the eating end off another wooden spoon and glue it to the back of the head so it sticks up from the top.

Edmontosaurus (ehd-MAHN-tuh-SAWR-uhs)

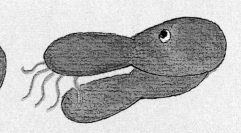

Corythosaurus Hat

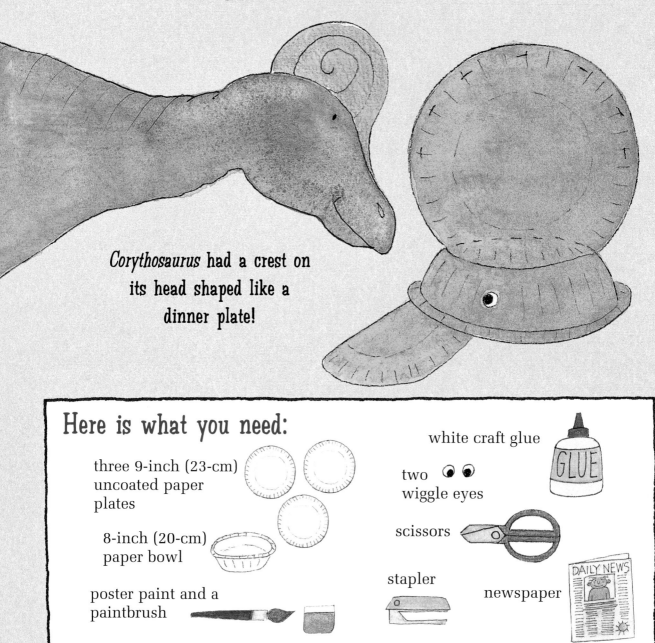

Corythosaurus had a crest on its head shaped like a dinner plate!

Here is what you need:

three 9-inch (23-cm) uncoated paper plates

8-inch (20-cm) paper bowl

poster paint and a paintbrush

white craft glue

two wiggle eyes

scissors

stapler

newspaper

Here is what you do:

1. Staple the two paper plates together as shown.

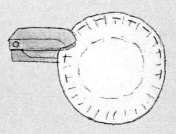

2. Fold the unstapled part of each plate out in the opposite direction.

3. Glue the bottom of the two folded-out edges to the bottom of the paper bowl.

4. Staple the last plate to the front part of the bowl to form the mouth of this duck-billed dinosaur.

5. Trim away the plate that is under the bowl.

6. Working on the newspaper, paint the dinosaur hat any way you want to. Nobody knows what color dinosaurs actually were.

7. Glue a wiggle eye on each side of the bowl below the crest.

Put on your hat, and pretend you are a Corythosaurus!

Corythosaurus (koh-RITH-uh-SAWR-uhs)

Parasaurolophus Puppet

Parasaurolophus, another duck-billed dinosaur, had a hollow bone running up the center of its face. It may have used this bone to trumpet calls to other dinosaurs.

Here is what you need:

adult-size sock

8-ounce (236-ml) plastic cup

two wiggle eyes

masking tape

cardboard party horn

white craft glue

GLUE

Here is what you do:

1. Tape the party horn to the side of the cup.

2. Glue on the wiggle eyes.

3. Line the inside of the cup with strips of masking tape to create a better gluing surface.

4. Glue the toe end of the sock inside the cup head. You may need to ask for help. Let dry.

Slip your hand into the sock. Blow on the party horn to make the Parasaurolophus *call to another dinosaur.*

Parasaurolophus (PAR-uh-SAWR-uh-LOH-fuhs)

Spinosaurus Magnet

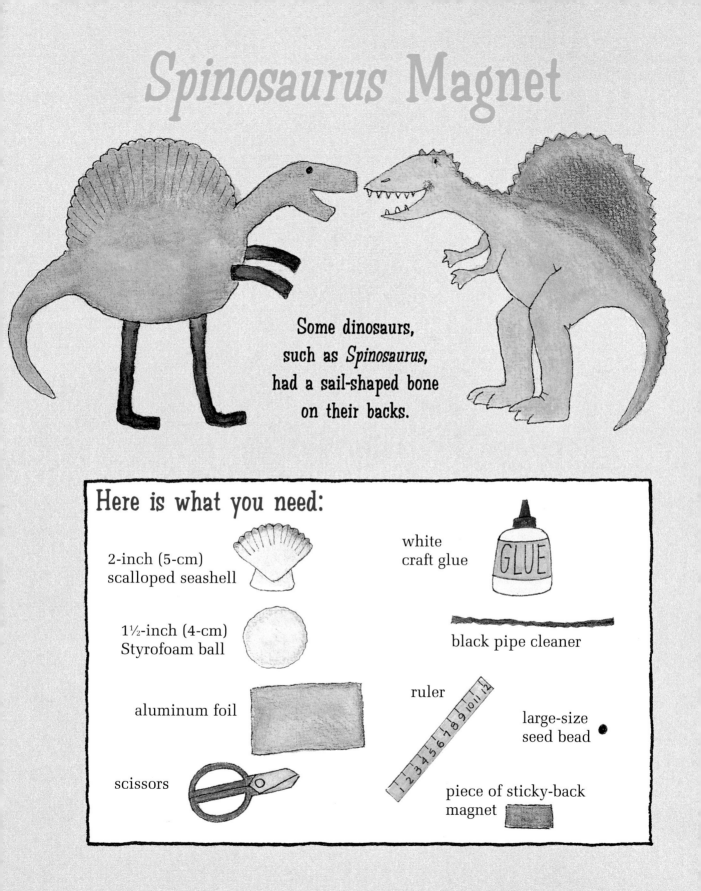

Some dinosaurs,
such as *Spinosaurus*,
had a sail-shaped bone
on their backs.

Here is what you need:

2-inch (5-cm)
scalloped seashell

1½-inch (4-cm)
Styrofoam ball

aluminum foil

scissors

white
craft glue

GLUE

black pipe cleaner

ruler

large-size
seed bead

piece of sticky-back
magnet

Here is what you do:

1. Tear off a strip of foil about 5 inches (13 cm) wide.

2. Press the base of the seashell into the Styrofoam ball.

3. Place the ball and seashell in the center of the foil strip. Wrap the foil around the ball and seashell.

4. Squeeze the extra foil together at each side of the ball.

5. Trim one end to about 2 inches (5 cm) long. This will be the head.

6. Cut the foil, and separate it to create a mouth.

7. Trim the other end 3 to 4 inches (8 to 10 cm) long. This will be the tail.

8. Squeeze the end of the foil into a point.

9. Cut four 2-inch (5-cm) pieces of the black pipe cleaner.

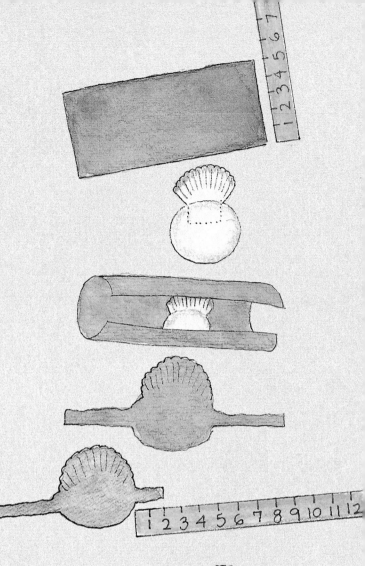

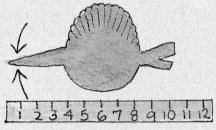

10. Press the ends of two of the pipe cleaner pieces through the foil and into the ball. These will be the legs.

11. Bend the ends of the legs forward to make feet.

12. Press the ends of the other two pieces of pipe cleaner into the ball below the head. These will be the arms.

13. Trim the arms so they are slightly shorter than the legs.

14. Glue the seed bead to the head for the eye.

15. Press a piece of sticky-back magnet to the back of the dinosaur.

Keep the Spinosaurus *on the refrigerator but don't let him in it! He is a hungry meat-eating dinosaur!*

Spinosaurus (SPY-nuh-SAWR-uhs)

Stegosaurus Scrap Box

Stegosaurus had large bony plates across its back.

Here is what you need:

two 9-inch (23-cm) white uncoated paper plates

large, empty tissue box

two clamp clothespins

scissors

stapler

white craft glue

small wiggle eye

paint and a paintbrush

newspaper

masking tape

Here is what you do:

1. Fold one paper plate in half. Secure the paper plate with a staple below the top rim.

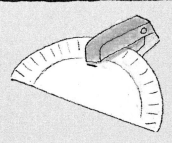

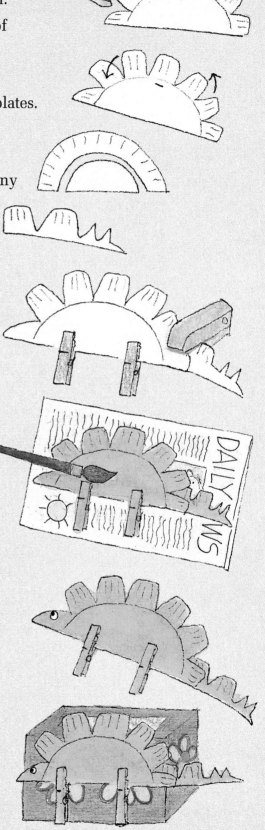

2. Cut a rounded head at one side of the rim. Cut 2-inch (5-cm) flaps along the entire rim of the folded paper plate.

3. Bend the flaps outward to form the bony plates.

4. Fold the second paper plate in half. Cut off the center. From the rim, cut two more bony plates and two points to make four spikes. This is the tail.

5. Staple the front end of the tail between the folds of the *Stegosaurus*.

6. Clamp two clothespins to the bottom of the body for legs.

7. Working on newspaper, paint the *Stegosaurus* any colors you want.

8. Glue the wiggle eye to the head.

9. Glue the *Stegosaurus* to the side of the tissue box.

10. You can cover any writing on the box with strips of masking tape or paint.

Keep the box on your desk or worktable for collecting small paper scraps.

Stegosaurus (STEG-uh-SAWR-uhs)

Hatching Baby Dinosaur

Scientists have found fossilized nests of baby dinosaur eggs.

Here is what you need:

plastic cup

3-inch (8-cm) piece of pipe cleaner

white craft glue

GLUE

black permanent marker

bump chenille stem

brown yarn bits

scissors

plastic straw

ballpoint pen

masking tape

ruler 1 2 3 4 5 6 7 8 9 10 11 12

Here is what you do:

1. Cut the cup about 1 inch (2.5 cm) from the base of the cup. The base will become the nest.

2. Cut a 2-inch (5-cm) piece from the plastic straw.

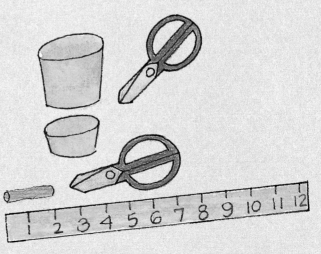

3. Wrap masking tape lightly around the straw to make an egg shape, leaving the ends uncovered.

4. Use the ballpoint pen to poke a hole through the bottom of the cup.

5. Glue the egg over the hole so the straw is over the cup opening. Make sure the holes are lined up.

6. Slip the remaining piece of pipe cleaner into the straw inside the egg and through the cup to keep the openings lined up until the glue has dried. Remove the pipe cleaner.

7. Make another egg by wrapping masking tape around itself in an oval shape. Make a third egg.

8. Glue the other eggs in the nest next to the first egg. Glue some yarn bits around the eggs.

9. Cut a bump from the chenille stem for the baby dinosaur head. Use the marker to draw eyes on each side of the head.

To hatch the baby dinosaur, push the chenille stem up through the hole in the bottom of the nest. The chenille stem will fluff out as it comes out of the egg.

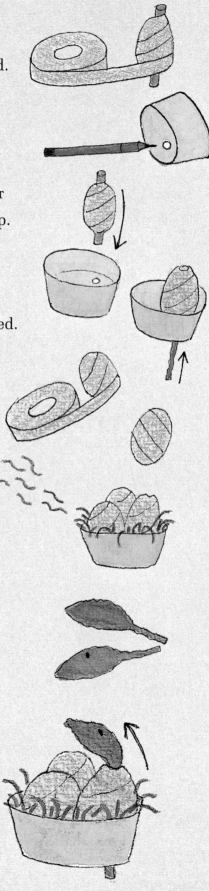

Pterodactyl Bookmark

Flying reptiles filled
the skies above
the dinosaurs.

Here is what you need:

brown mailing
envelope

two 12-inch (30-cm)
pipe cleaners

black
permanent
marker

scissors

masking tape

ruler

Here is what you do:

1. Cut a triangle with a 6-inch (15-cm) base
from the corner of the brown envelope.

2. Cut the open end of the triangle into
a slight curve to form the wings.

3. Fold one of the pipe cleaners in half.
Bend the folded end out to shape a head.

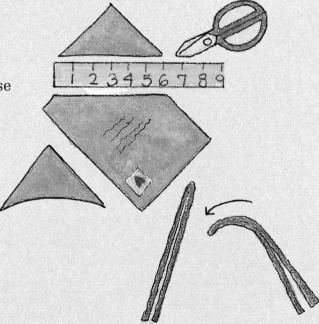

4. Use the marker to draw eyes.

5. Cut a small piece from the tip of the triangle wings opposite the open end to create a hole.

6. Slide the head up into the triangle wings and through the hole in the tip.

7. Fold the two ends of the pipe cleaner out to shape the feet.

8. Tape the pipe cleaner legs to the front inside of the triangle wings. Keep the tape as smooth as possible.

9. Cut a 6-inch (15-cm) piece from the second pipe cleaner to make the arms.

10. Snip a tiny hole about halfway down each side of the wings.

11. Thread the piece of pipe cleaner through the two holes. A piece should stick out on each side. Fold the ends around.

12. Tape the pipe cleaner to the front inside of the wings.

To use the bookmark, slip the pterodactyl *over the corner of the page in your book that you want to mark.*

Pterodactyl (tehr-uh-DAK-tul)

Pteranodon Lapel Pin

This *Pteranodon* wants to fly with you!

Here is what you need:

old necktie

tiny wiggle eye

scissors

thin pipe cleaner

white craft glue

safety pin

ruler

Here is what you do:

1. Cut a triangle with a 3-inch (8-cm) base from the tip of the old necktie.

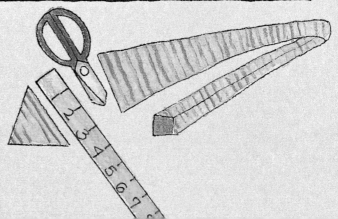

2. Cut the base in a slight curve.

3. Fold a 6-inch (15-cm) piece of pipe cleaner in half. Bend the ends out to form feet.

4. Cut a tiny opening at the tip of the necktie wings. Slip the folded end of the pipe cleaner up through the hole about 1 inch (2.5 cm).

5. Fold the tip of the pipe cleaner to form the crest.

6. Glue the pipe cleaner to the necktie at the neck. Use very little glue, or you will stain the tie fabric.

7. Cut a 2-inch (5-cm) piece from the remaining pipe cleaner. Wrap it around the folded pipe cleaner just below the crest for the head. Trim the ends so that they are ¾ inch (2 cm) long.

8. Glue on a wiggle eye.

9. Pin a safety pin to the back of the *Pteranodon*.

Pin the Pteranodon *to the collar of your coat or shirt.*

Pteranodon (tehr-RAN-uh-dahn)

Dinosaur Toss Ball

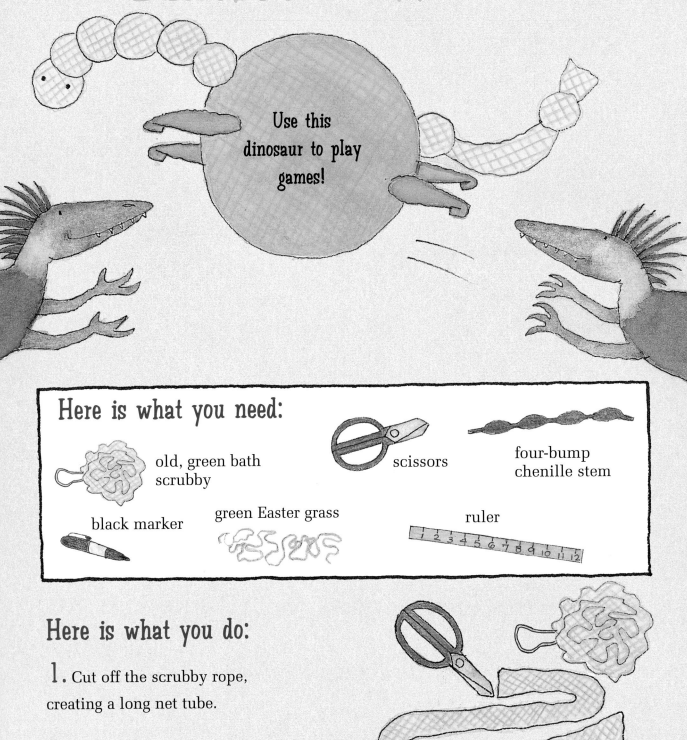

Use this dinosaur to play games!

Here is what you need:

old, green bath scrubby

scissors

four-bump chenille stem

black marker

green Easter grass

ruler

Here is what you do:

1. Cut off the scrubby rope, creating a long net tube.

2. Cut a 30-inch (76-cm) piece from the net tube.

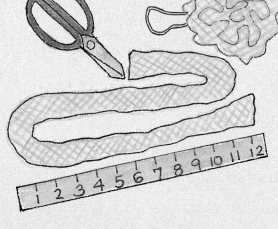

3. Tie a knot in the end of the tube.

4. Tie a second knot about 6 inches (15 cm) from the first knot. This will be the tail for the dinosaur.

5. Stuff the tube with Easter grass until you have a round body about 5 inches (13 cm) across.

6. Tie the tube in a knot to secure the grass body. Make several knots at the front of the tube to create the neck and head.

7. Trim off any extra net.

8. Use the marker to draw eyes.

9. Cut the bump chenille stem in half. Thread each stem through the net at the bottom of the dinosaur. These will be the legs. Fold the wire tips over so they are not sharp.

Try throwing the dinosaur ball into a bucket or through a hole cut in a hanging paper plate. What other games can you think of to play with your dinosaur ball?

Stuffed Dinosaur Pet

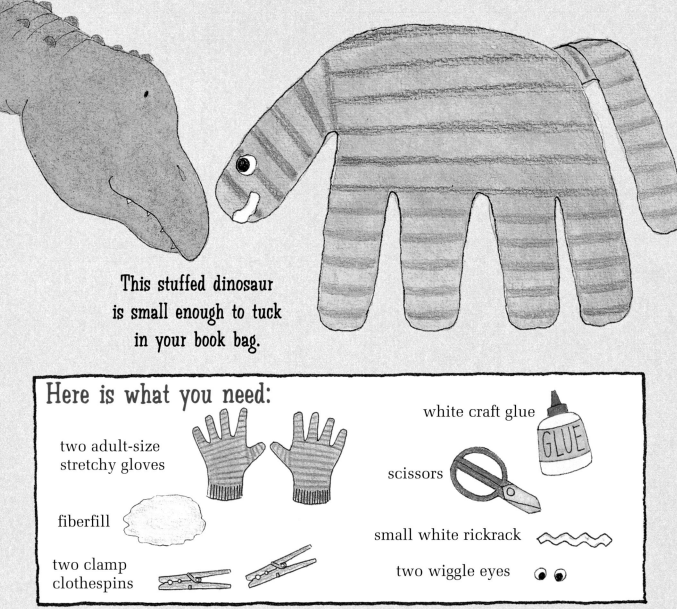

This stuffed dinosaur
is small enough to tuck
in your book bag.

Here is what you need:

two adult-size
stretchy gloves

fiberfill

two clamp
clothespins

white craft glue

scissors

small white rickrack

two wiggle eyes

Here is what you do:

1. Lightly stuff each finger of the glove with
fiberfill. Then stuff the thumb and palm.

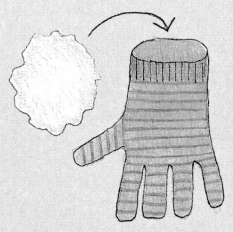

2. Cut a tail for the dinosaur from the second glove, by cutting off the last finger up to the cuff.

3. Turn the cuff inside the first glove, and glue the two sides together to close the glove.

4. Tuck the cuff end of the tail into the glued cuff at the end opposite the thumb.

5. Secure the glued cuff with the clamp clothespins until the glue has dried.

6. Glue a wiggle eye on each side of the thumb.

7. Cut a 1-inch (2.5-cm) piece of the white rickrack.

8. Glue the rickrack to the thumb below the eyes for teeth.

By using a child-size stretchy glove, you can make a dinosaur baby for your new pet.

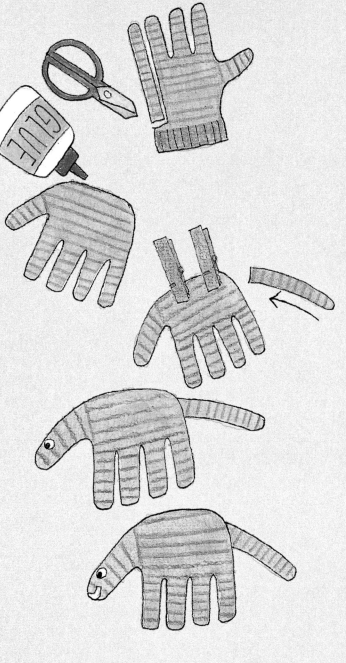

Quick Cup Dinosaur

Make a whole herd of long-necked dinosaurs in no time!

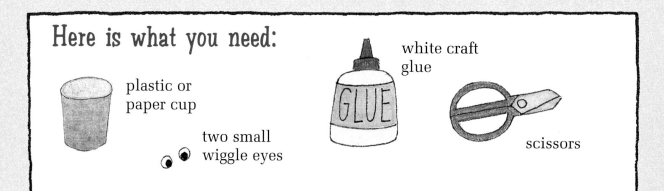

Here is what you need:

plastic or
paper cup

two small
wiggle eyes

white craft
glue

scissors

Here is what you do:

1. Starting at the rim, cut to two-thirds
of the way up the cup.

2. Make a second cut about 1 inch (2.5 cm) from the first cut.

3. Fold the tab out from the cup. Round off the end by cutting it with the scissors. This is the head.

4. Make an identical tab on the opposite side of the cup.

5. Fold the tab out, and cut the end into a point for the tail.

6. Cut out an arched section on each side of the cup to make legs.

7. Glue on the wiggle eyes.

Use cups of different sizes and colors to create a whole collection of different dinosaurs.

Dinosaur Tape Dispenser

Turn an ordinary tape dispenser into a dinosaur.

Here is what you need:

white craft glue

clear plastic
tape dispenser

scissors

green construction
paper

wiggle eye

pen

Here is what you do:

1. Pop the tape out of the tape dispenser.

2. Remove the paper liner.

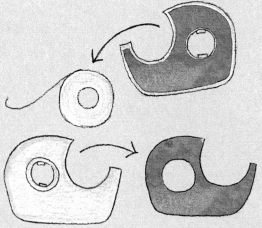

3. Using the liner as a pattern, trace the shape on the green construction paper. Cut the shape out.

4. Place the shape inside the tape dispenser as the liner.

5. Pop the tape back into the dispenser.

6. Stand the tape dispenser on end with the cutting edge on top to become the teeth of the dinosaur.

7. Glue the wiggle eye to the dispenser behind the "teeth."

8. Cut a haunch and leg shape from the green paper. Glue the piece over the hole in the dispenser.

9. Cut a long tail from the green paper. Glue the top of the tail to the dinosaur so it hangs down.

This craft is a perfect gift for your favorite paleontologist. (A paleontologist is a scientist who studies dinosaurs!)

About the Author and Artist

With more than one million copies of her books in print, **Kathy Ross** has written over fifty titles and her name has become synonymous with "top quality craft books." Following twenty five years of developing nursery school programs and guiding young children through craft projects, Ross has authored many successful series, including *Crafts for Kids Who Are Learning about . . .*, *Girl Crafts*, and *All New Holiday Crafts for Kids*.

Jan Barger's favorite present as a child was a thick pad of paper and a big box of crayons, and she still gets that same excitement from paper and paints. When she is not illustrating, she enjoys singing in choirs and playing the flute and piccolo. She lives in Plumpton, England, with her husband and their cocker spaniel, Tosca.

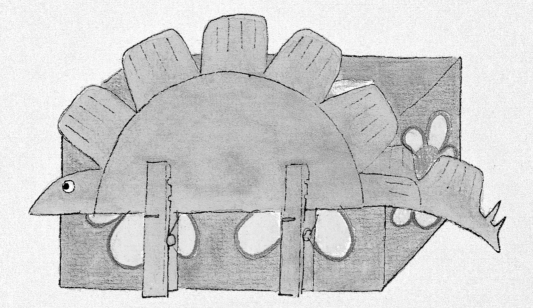